THE
BOSTON COMMONS
QUILT

BLANCHE YOUNG & HELEN YOUNG

ACKNOWLEDGEMENTS

Our deepest thanks to the many people that contributed their time and talents to this book; to our friends and students for allowing us to photograph their quilts; to Mary Anne Johnson for technical advice; to Doris Crutchfield for her help; and to Verna Brightwell, Mary Andra Holmes, Monette Utz, and The Four Seasons Quilters for their Quilting Bee stitches. We acknowledge with gratitude the extra efforts of Debbie Gordon and Beverly Packard.

Our gratitude to our Colorado friends for the use of their quilts; Mary Anne Johnson, Sandra Schwartz, and Genevieve Salazar.

A special thanks to Tom Frost for always having the right word, and to Lynette Young Bingham for her extraordinary skills. We are also most grateful for the support we received from Dallas and the family.

Published by C&T Publishing, P.O. Box 1456
Lafayette, CA 94549

ISBN: 0-914881-17-5

Copyright©1983 by Blanche Young and Helen Young

THE
BOSTON COMMONS
QUILT

Other books by the authors
The Lone Star Quilt Handbook
Trip Around the World Quilts
The Flying Geese Quilt

CONTENTS

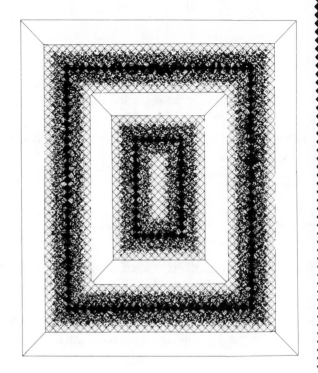

The *Boston Commons* quilt is a traditional design. A center rectangle of patchwork squares is bordered with plain fabric, bordered again with patchwork and finished with another plain border. This series of borders make it easy to understand the quilts' name; Boston Common in Boston, Massachusetts is itself a series of borders of park and pavement.

However, the quilt is usually made as a scrap quilt. Solid color squares separated the white borders from the patchwork, which was usually an assortment of prints randomly placed.

We have updated the design of the quilt and the method of its construction. We applied the same ideas and techniques that we developed and presented in our book *Trip Around The World Quilts*. This method makes use of purchased fabrics (not scraps) a multiple template for cutting rows of squares instead of individual squares, and repeated fabric arrangements. We have translated this "scrap" quilt into a stately, formal design that now closer identifies with the city of its name.

To form an interesting design utilizing several fabrics, we have used very small squares in these quilts. We try to keep the size of the square in proportion to the size of the quilt. They range from 1¼ inch for the wall quilt to a 2 inch square for the king-size quilt. Most sizes use squares that measure 1¾ inches. These quilts require patience and a great deal of sewing! This book offers an efficient way to cut and sew these quilts but they should not be considered fast or easy.

The *Boston Commons* quilt offers the quilter an opportunity to show off her skills. The plain borders will display any quilting design to advantage.

After teaching this quilt for some time, we realized that we had not allowed enough length in the sizes. The quilts in the color sections will not have the same number of center squares as the sewing layouts.

In the special pocket at the back of the book, you will find a ready to cut and use multiple template sheet. We have also included several different quilting patterns that have been designed to fit the borders of these quilts.

It is our hope that you will use and enjoy this book as much as you will enjoy your *Boston Commons* quilt.

Markers   Use a pencil or dressmakers chalk pencil to mark the fabrics.

Scissors   Very good, sharp scissors are a must. Use paper scissors for cutting the template.

Ruler   You will need a 12 inch ruler, a yardstick or tape measure.

Tape   Use frosted scotch tape. This will be used on the fabric.

Pins   Extra-long glass headed dressmakers or quilters pins work best when pinning through several layers of fabric.

Thread   Use a good quality thread in a medium shade of the colors in the quilt.

Spray Starch   The fabrics will mark easier, shift less during cutting, and handle better during the sewing if spray starch is used during pressing.

Needles   Use betweens needles in sizes 8, 9, 10 or 12; milliners or sharps for basting.

Batting   Quilt batting is sold in packages by the quilt size. Bonded polyester batting is sold by the yard and requires piecing. We prefer traditional weights in the packaged batting, and 3 ounce batting by the yard.

Frames/ Hoops   Personal preference will determine whether frames or a quilt hoop is used. The quilt must be thoroughly basted before quilting on a hoop.

Sewing machine   The method was developed for machine piecing.

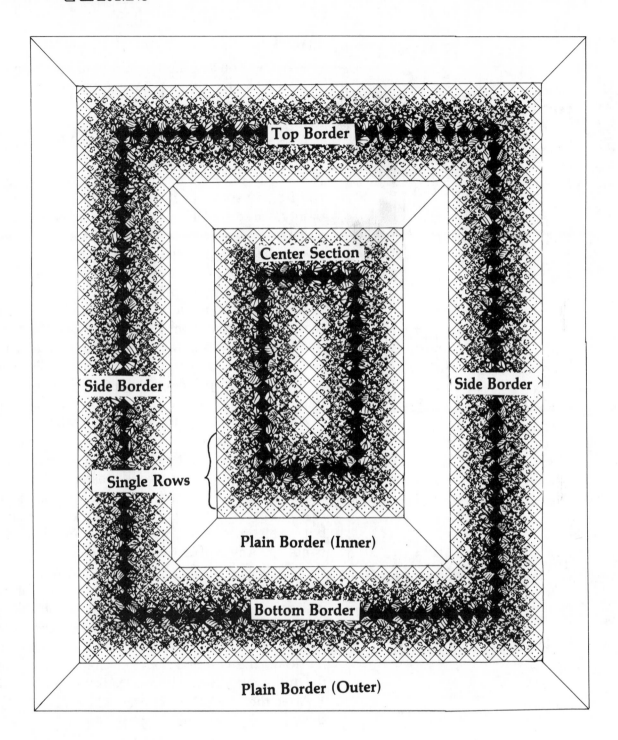

Top Border

Center Section

Side Border

Side Border

Single Rows

Plain Border (Inner)

Bottom Border

Plain Border (Outer)

The size of the quilt is determined by the diagonal measurement of the sewn square.

Square size (sewn)	Diagonal	
	Decimal	Fractional
1-1/4"	1.77	1-3/4
1-1/2"	2.12	2-1/8
1-3/4"	2.47	2-1/2
2"	2.83	2-7/8

An assortment of prints

Too much background

Avoid one-way prints

Fabrics

Whether you are shopping at your local quilt shop or fabric store, or rummaging through your own fabric collection at home, here are a few guidelines to help you select fabrics for your quilt.

Choose an assortment of prints. Mix florals and paisleys with dots and geometric designs. Look for prints with different amounts of background. Florals can be tiny sprigs of flowers to almost life-size. Use dainty, soft prints that appear to be a plain color from a distance. A mixture of prints in design and scale will always be more interesting than using prints that are similar. Choose fabrics for their overall effect when combined with other prints.

The *Boston Commons* quilt is made with squares that range in size from 1¼ to 2 inches. Keep this in mind when selecting fabrics that have large areas of background. Each square should show a little of the print. One-way prints or stripes are not suitable for these quilts since the squares are on the diagonal.

Although we tend to choose our fabrics by color and print, we should not forget how important fiber content is. Most quilters prefer 100% cotton broad-cloth weight fabrics for a good reason. Cotton fabrics handle better during marking and sewing and press easier. Polyester and cotton blends are also suitable but sometimes have a tendency to shift during handling. Any fabrics that are very lightweight, loose woven, or fray easily should be avoided.

All yardages are figured for 42 inch wide fabric (45 inch fabric minus selvages) to allow for shrinkage or crooked edges. All border yardages are figured for the lengthwise grain of the fabric. This will leave extra fabric on the width. When figuring the yardage for the quilts, we allowed two extra rows on each fabric.

After the fabrics are chosen, they should be pre-shrunk and pressed using spray starch.

Design

Traditionally, the *Boston Commons* quilt was a scrap quilt. Solid color squares outlined the borders, but all the others were assorted scraps randomly placed. All of the quilts we are presenting here were made with the fabrics in a reverse repeat sequence. That is, the fabrics were used once then repeated in reverse in both the center section and the border. This forms a balanced, orderly design which is even more attractive when the quilt is on the bed. This also allows us to figure accurate yardage requirements. Only the wall quilt does not repeat the fabric in the border.

We prefer arranging the fabric lightest to darkest to reinforce the design. The darkest fabric in the border usually follows the edge of the bed. This light to dark fabric arrangement can be monochromatic as in Ellen Benke's wall quilt in Plate 9. Two or more colors can be combined and still have a light to dark arrangement. Ruth Greene's quilt in Plate 7 is a good example of this. When selecting fabrics for a light to dark arrangement, avoid prints with a very light figure on a very dark background. A print like this will refuse to blend.

Fabrics can also be arranged in a complementary order instead of light to dark. In the quilt on the back cover (upper right) Monette Utz placed the rust and blue fabrics so they would complement each other.

Once the fabrics and arrangement are chosen, cut and tape a small swatch of each to a piece of paper. Number the fabrics in order.

The plain fabric that is used for the borders is also used for the first squares of the patchwork sections. These squares are trimmed in half when the borders are added. To help the border seams be less noticeable, the first print should be very close in color to the plain fabric. Both the quilt on the cover and Eleanor Haywood's quilt in Plate 2 have fabrics that achieve the effect of the squares blending into the borders. Some people prefer to have the squares contrast with the plain fabric, forming a zig-zag edge to the border. To do this, the plain fabric must be much lighter than the first print, as in Genevieve Salazar's wall quilt on the back cover, or much darker, as in Doris Carmack's quilt in Plate 13.

Reverse repeat sequence

The squares blending
into the plain borders

The squares contrasting
with the plain border

11

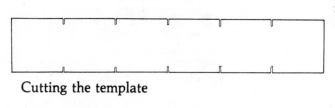

Cutting the template

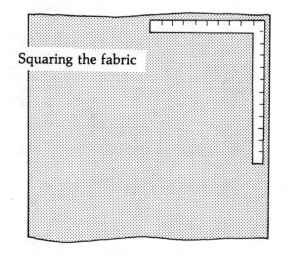

Squaring the fabric

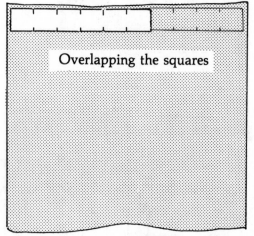

Overlapping the squares

Marking

To make sure your quilt is the right size, it is always a good idea to measure the bed beforehand. Mattress sizes are standard, but bed heights are not. The sizes of the quilts can be changed by adding to the outer plain border or eliminating it.

Carefully cut out the multiple templates found in the pocket at the back of the book. Cut the notches out, leaving space for a pencil point. The sizes of the quilts and the yardage requirements are based on the size of square listed with each quilt. Double check to make sure the template size is correct.

Square the fabric by drawing a line perpendicular to the selvage. An L-square ruler, or anything with a true right angle will work. Place this next to the selvage and draw a line across the full width of the fabric.

Mark the squares on *Fabric 1*. Always place another fabric beneath for stability. Place the template on the line, ½ inch away from the selvage. Mark the long edges of the template, then mark in the notches. Don't mark around the left-hand end of the template yet. Overlap the template on the marked squares, matching the notches and continue marking. Continue overlapping until a row of squares is marked across the width of the fabric. Mark the next row under the first, using the common line between them. Continue until the needed number of rows are marked. Each quilt lists the number of rows to mark instead of the number of squares. Since some fabrics are narrower, the full number of squares may not be reached. Mark an extra row to make up for this.

Each row should contain:

size of square	number of squares
1¼	23
1½	20
1¾	18
2	16

Marking the rows

Cutting

Several layers of fabrics can be cut together with good scissors. If your scissors will not cut all the layers accurately, then you must mark the needed number of rows on another fabric and cut them in two groups.

Layer the fabrics in order, keeping their right-hand selvages even. Place the marked layer on top so the squares are on all the layers. The bottom fabric will be shorter than the rest.

Pin through the layers using 5 or 6 pins on each row. Cut the rows out carefully, keeping the scissors straight. Trim off the excess at the sides and top.

To transfer the marks, snip the notches, keeping the scissors straight. Cut only ¼ inch deep, through all the fabrics. *Do not cut into squares.* These notches, or snips, are all that is needed to indicate the outline of each square. Do not move or shift the rows while snipping the notches. Trim off any incomplete squares caused by narrower fabrics. Separate the layers and group the fabrics in sequence.

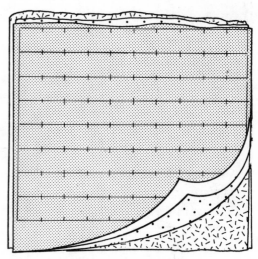

Layering the fabrics

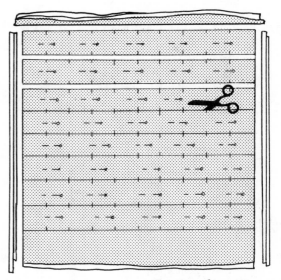

Cutting the rows

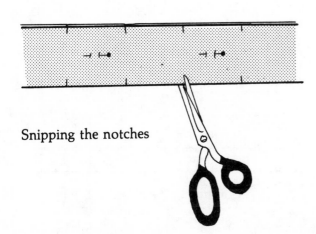

Snipping the notches

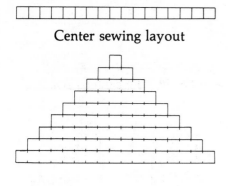

Center sewing layout

Border sewing layout

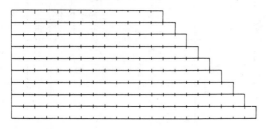

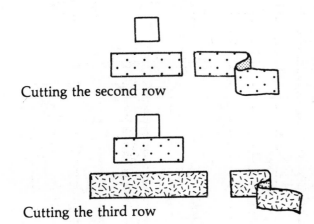

Cutting the second row

Cutting the third row

Cutting from notch to notch

Stacking

The *Boston Commons* quilt is made in sections as the diagram on Page 9 illustrates. The center has two identical sections and one or more single rows. The border consists of identical side sections and identical top and bottom sections. Make two sections from each sewing layout.

Each row in the center sewing layout increases by one square on each side. Cut a single square from *Fabric 1*. Place a row of *Fabric 2* next to it. Cut the row so there is one square extending on each side. Continue in this manner using the fabrics in order. Always cut straight from notch to notch.

As each row is cut, it can be placed on top of the previous rows. That is why we refer to this step as "stacking."

Some rows will require more squares than the width of the fabric will yield. To continue a row, place the ends together and tape. This tape will be removed after the rows are sewn.

The border sections are also cut and stacked before sewing. Count the number of squares in the top row. Each successive row will extend one square on the right-hand side.

Since the sections are identical, they can be stacked at the same time, next to each other. This reduces the number of times each fabric is handled.

After all the sections are stacked, pin the layers together for transporting to the sewing machine.

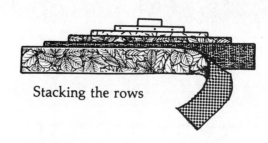

Stacking the rows

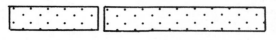

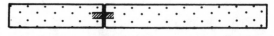

Continuing the rows with tape

Sewing

Place the stacked rows on a table or other flat sur-face to the right side of the sewing machine. Leave the rows in the order they were stacked, with the longest row on top. Begin sewing with this row.

Sew with a consistent ¼ inch seam allowance, using 12 to 15 stitches per inch. Begin and end the stitching ¼ inch beyond the notches instead of backstitching.

Sew the rows, then open them right side up. Place the next row on top and sew, matching the notches. These notches will be the guide for cutting the rows apart, so they *must* match. The notches can be pinned, or the rows can be held so the notches match. Sometimes a tight weave fabric needs to be stretched slightly when it is joined to a loose weave fabric.

Continue until all the rows are joined. The sewn rows will duplicate the sewing layout. Repeat for the second half of the center section.

Always begin sewing the border sections with the longest row. Each successive row will have one less square. It is important that the rows are sewn in this order. The staggered edge should be on the right-hand side of the section when it is face up. This will make the following steps easier.

Continue until all the rows are added. The sewn rows will duplicate the sewing layout.

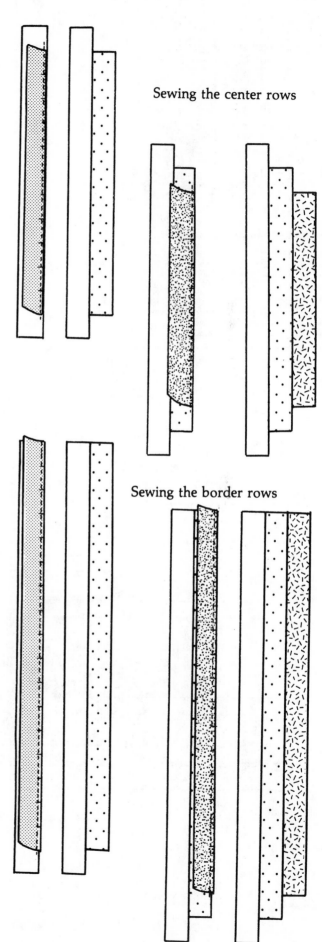

Sewing the center rows

Sewing the border rows

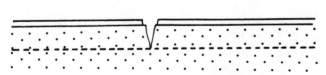

Matching the snipped notches

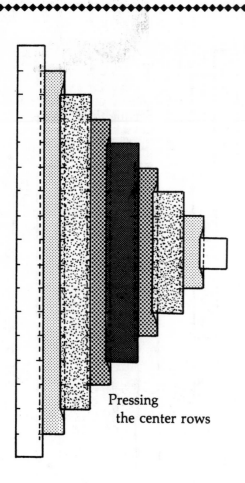

Pressing
the center rows

Pressing

The seam allowances are pressed to one side, with the directions alternated. Begin by pressing away from the outside edges. The seams will face opposite directions when the rows are cut apart and resewn. Many quilters find that their seams match better in the corners when the seams are opposite each other like this. This method requires less pinning since the seams can just be held together as they are sewn. You will be able to quilt next to the seams, but there will be some bulkiness at each corner.

You might want to consider the alternate method of pressing the seams open. This is not traditional in patchwork, but we've found that it will help the patchwork look smooth and uniform, especially with the small squares of the wall quilt. Pressing the seams open will take much longer than pressing to one side. Each seam will have to be pinned during the sewing. Having the seams open reduces the bulk in the corners of the squares. It is easier to quilt from corner to corner with the seams like this.

Remove all the tape before pressing. Press with a light touch but make sure the seams are flat.

Pressing
the border rows

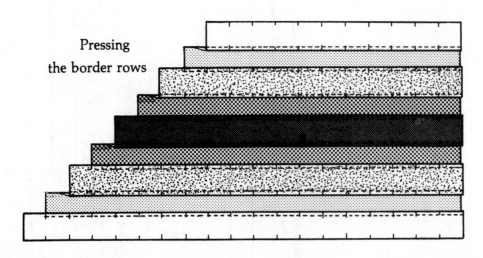

2 In progress quilt by Eleanor Haywood.

1 This wall quilt (36″ × 40″) by Mary Anne Johnson would be the focal point of any room.

3 Quilt top by Sandy Pigford.

4 Quilt top by Blanche Young.

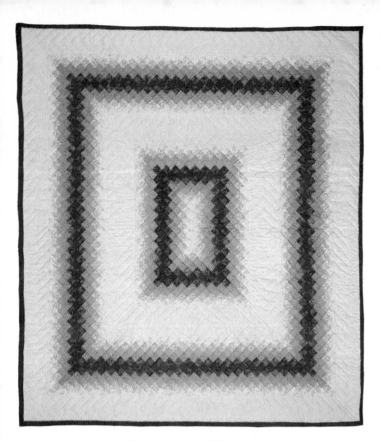

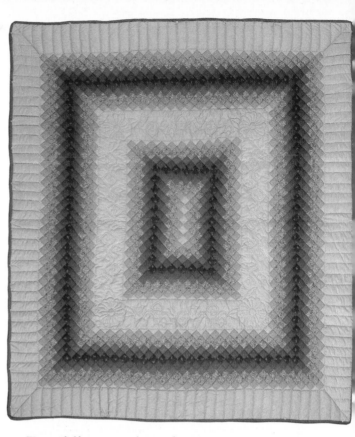

5 Simple lines of quilting highlight this quilt (102″ × 112″) by Virginia Nicholson.

6 Two different quilting designs are used in this quilt (90″ × 102″) by Teen Keith.

7 The *Boston Commons* quilt design effectively displays elegant quilting in this quilt (102″ × 107″) by Ruth Greene.

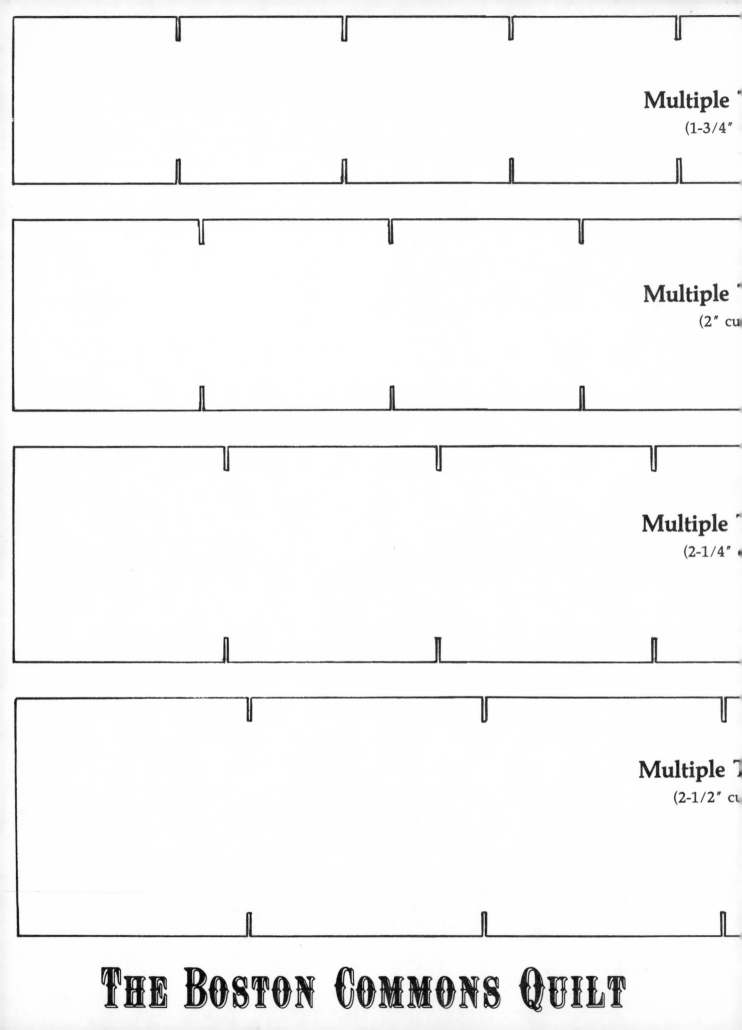

Multiple T
(1-3/4″

Multiple T
(2″ cu

Multiple T
(2-1/4″

Multiple T
(2-1/2″ cu

THE BOSTON COMMONS QUILT

8 Baby quilt (42″ × 47″) by Helen Young, quilted by Beverly Packard.

9 Wall quilt (36″ × 40″) by Ellen Benke shows subtle gradations of shades of blue.

10 *Winter Sunset Over Boston Commons* (36″ × 40″) by Sandra Schwartz was inspired by the colors of the Colorado sunset.

11 Baby quilt by Helen Young, quilted by Debbie Gordon.

15 Wall quilt by Blanche Young.

12 (upper left) Quilt by Dorothy Hines.

13 (center left) Quilt top by Doris Carmack.

14 (lower left) Twin size quilt top by Helen Young.

16 In progress quilt by Blanche Young.

Cutting

The sections are now cut into rows of squares. Spread each section face down on a table. The notches indicate the cutting line. Cut from notch to notch crossing each square with one stroke. Or use a ruler to draw a line from notch to notch, and then cut on the line.

As the rows are cut, place them face down in order with the top edges even. The first row is actually just one square. Each row increases in length until the center, then they will decrease. Pin securely to keep the rows in order.

Place each border section face down with the longest row at the bottom. Cut apart into rows of squares, placing them face down in order with their top edges even. The rows will be the same length until the end, when they begin to decrease. Continue to place them in order, with the top edges even. Pin them together at the top.

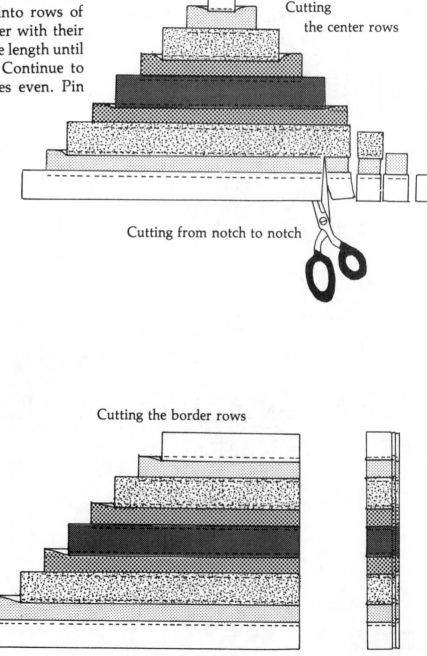

Cutting the center rows

Cutting from notch to notch

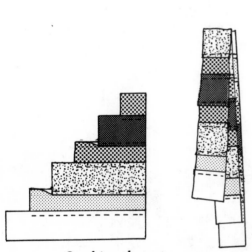

Stacking the cut rows

Cutting the border rows

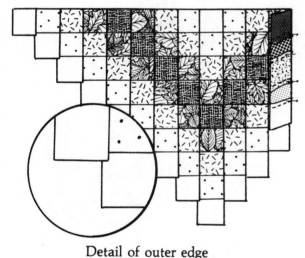

Sewing the center sections

Detail of outer edge

Sewing the Center

Leave the cut rows face down, being careful not to disturb their order. Take the first square from the stack and turn it face up. The next row is placed face down with its top edge even with the first square. Sew with a consistent ¼ inch seam allowance, extending the stitching ¼ inch instead of backstitching. Open, then place the next row face down and sew. Each row will increase in length until the center, then they will decrease. At the end of each row, the last square will extend ¼ inch. This will be part of the seam allowance when the plain borders are added.

There is tendency for this second set of seams to be slightly larger than the first. This will result in squares that are slightly rectangular and the sections will be distorted. Stop every few rows and measure the squares from the front to check that the seams are consistent.

The seams will face opposite directions at each corner and can be held against each other as they are sewn. Be aware that some sewing machines can drag the top layer slightly while easing in the bottom layer. Prevent this by pinning the seams in place. Always pin perpendicular to the seams.

After the center sections are sewn, press in alternate directions as shown.

Measuring the squares

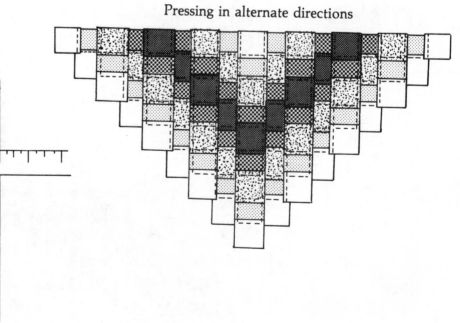

Pressing in alternate directions

Sewing the Single Rows

The finished center sections are the diagonal halves of the center section of the quilt. The only way to lengthen this section is to add single rows. These are each offset one square.

The wall quilt and baby quilt have one single row. These are made by sewing individual squares into a row. Follow the fabric numbers in the sewing layouts.

The other quilt sizes use five or more single rows. These can be made most easily by using the same techniques as the other sections. Cut off the necessary number of squares indicated in the sewing layouts. Sew, matching the notches, and press as shown. Cut apart, using the notches as the cutting line. Place face down on top of each other. To sew, simply offset the rows by one square. Continue until all the single rows are joined. The completed center sections are added to the single rows to form the center patchwork section of the quilt. Press these last seams.

Since the squares are all set on the diagonal, the lengthwise grain of the fabric is at an angle in the quilt. The grainline in the single rows will run the opposite direction. Even with polished fabrics this grainline change is not apparent. Only one-way prints will show the change. If stripes or other one-way prints have been used, the single rows must be constructed one at a time, by sewing individual squares together.

Lengthening the center with single rows

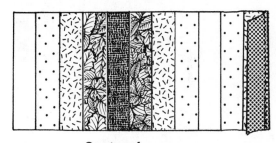

Sewing the rows

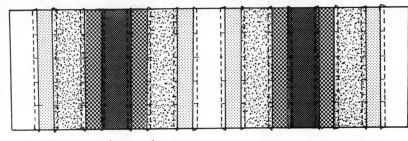

Pressing the single rows

Offsetting the single rows

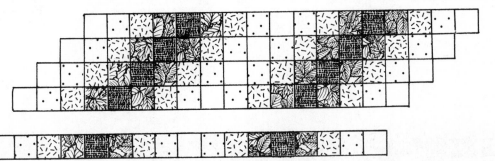

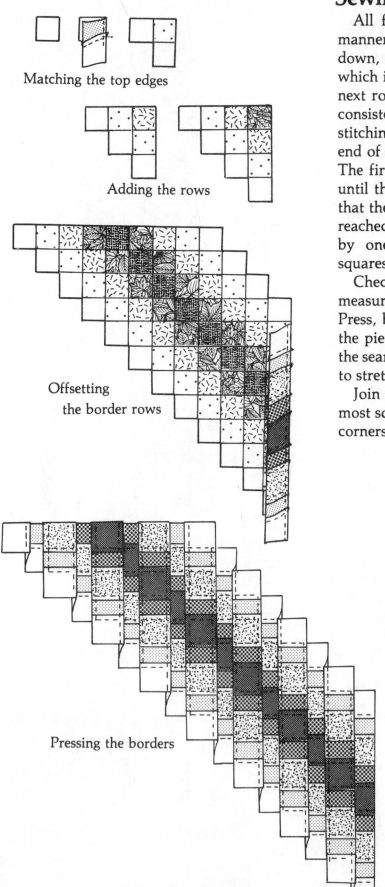

Matching the top edges

Adding the rows

Offsetting
the border rows

Pressing the borders

Sewing the Borders

All four border sections are pieced in the same manner. Begin by placing the stacked rows face down, just as they were cut. Remove the first row, which is a single square, and turn it face up. Sew the next row to it, with the top edges even. Sew with a consistent ¼ inch seam allowance, extending the stitching at the end instead of backstitching. At the end of each row, the last square will extend ¼ inch. The first few rows increase in length by one square until the rows contain the entire fabric repeat. After that they remain the same length. When that point is reached, the rows must be dropped down, or offset, by one square. Continue adding the rows. The squares will extend ¼ inch at the top and bottom.

Check the accuracy of the seam allowance by measuring the squares from the front every few rows. Press, beginning with the first seam. Press it towards the piece, and continue to alternate the direction of the seams. Press with a gentle touch since it is possible to stretch and distort the sections because of the bias.

Join the four border sections, noting that the outermost squares of the top and bottom sections form the corners.

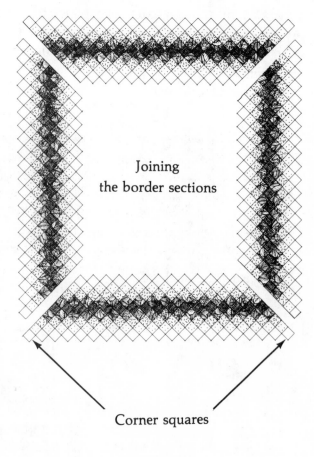

Joining
the border sections

Corner squares

24

Measuring for Plain Borders

After some experimenting, we realized that the width of the plain borders could not be just any size. If the squares edging the plain border are to be opposite each other, the plain border size must be a multiple of the diagonal measurement of the square. It should be as if several rows of squares were removed and replaced with plain fabric. And for the plain border to be in proportion with the patchwork, we found that the width should be the same as one fourth of the width of the center section.

Count the number of squares that span the width. These squares are diagonal and they touch corners only. The wall and baby quilts' centers are eight squares wide, so the borders will be 2 diagonal squares. The other quilts' centers are 12 squares wide, so the borders will be three diagonal squares wide.

Instead of multiplying the number of squares by the diagonal measurement, *measure your quilt.* This will give the proper measurement in case your seams were slightly larger or smaller. Add ½ inch to the measurement for seams.

Here are the approximate sizes of the borders:

Measuring the diagonal
of the squares

Quilt size	Width of border
Wall quilt (using 1¼″ squares)	3½″
Wall quilt (using 1½″ squares)	4¼″
Baby quilt	4¼″
Twin, Double/Queen	7½″
King	8½″

To find the length of the borders, measure the center section and add the width of the border twice, then add ½ inch for seams. Measure through the middle of the center section, not the outside edges since they can stretch. Measure from the outer tips of the second row of squares.

Measure and mark the four inner borders. After cutting the borders, fold the ends as shown and press. This crease will mark the miter seams.

Measuring for the length
of the plain borders

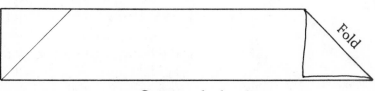

Creasing the borders

Marking the diagonal size
of the square on the plain border

Pinning
the plain border to the squares

Attaching
the plain borders

Mitering
the plain borders

Sewing the Plain Borders

Sewing the plain borders to the completed patch-work sections is trickier than it appears. The seams will be on the bias of the squares so some precautions must be taken against the squares stretching. We have found that staystitching through the squares is not a solution. There is a tendency for the bias edges to stretch even more or pull in too tightly. For the squares to match across the plain border, they must stay their actual size. We have always realized it is much easier to trim off the outer half of the squares *after* all the borders are added.

The most careful approach is to mark the diagonal measurement of your squares on the borders. This is much simpler than it sounds! Gently spread the completed center section face up on a table. Place the plain border piece face down on it as if to sew. Since the outside edges may have already stretched slightly, move the border so its edge crosses the centers of the *Fabric 3* squares. Make a mark on the border where the corners of the *Fabric 3* squares connect. A small mark in the seam allowance is all that is needed. Transfer these marks to the other edges with a ruler. Place the border back on the patchwork to finish marking the outer ends. Pin the corners of the squares to each of these marks. The center of the last square should be pinned to the crease in the border.

Another approach consists of careful pinning instead of marking. Fold the plain border in half to find the center. This will be pinned to the center of the edge of the patchwork (find the center by counting the squares). Pin the ends, then in between. The pins at the ends should be through the crease in the border and through the center of the last square. This method simply evenly distributes any fullness.

Most sewing machines tend to ease in the bottom layer of fabric. To take advantage of this, have the center section (with its bias edges) on the bottom and the border piece on top. However, you will not be able to see the squares. Follow the pins at the corners of each square or use your fingers to feel where the tip of each square is. You want to avoid sewing too deep and "losing" the corner of the square in the seam.

Sewing with the squares on top and the border on the bottom will allow you to follow the squares as a guide. However, you will be sewing on the bias of the top fabric. This can cause problems if your sewing machine tends to drag the top layer. There may be extra fabric that will have to be eased in at the end. Marking a sewing line through the squares will help keep the seams straight.

Always sew with a consistent ¼ inch seam allowance, beginning and ending the seam at the crease in the border. Backstitch just two or three stitches at the start and stop of each seam. Pin and sew one border section at a time.

To miter the borders, align the creases and pin. Sew from the outside edge in towards the piece. Trim the excess fabric then press the miter seams open.

One small preparation must be made on the patchwork borders before they can be added. In the four inside corners, the seams need to end on the sewing line of the square. Remove the extending stitches and backstitch, by hand or machine, on the sewing line of the square. Fold the corners of the plain borders until the folded edge measures the same as the square plus seams. Mark by creasing. Sew these four inside corner seams, matching the sewing line of the square to the crease. Sew from seam to seam as shown.

Attach the border sections to the plain borders pinning and sewing as before. Begin and end the stitching at the corner square seams.

The outer plain borders will be the same width as the inner plain borders. To determine their length, measure the quilt. Always measure through the center instead of at the edges. This gives a truer measurement. Measure from the outer corners of the second row of squares. Add the width of the border twice, then add ½ inch for seams. Cut the borders, then fold the ends and press. The crease will mark the miter seam. The outer plain borders are sewn and mitered in the same manner as the inner borders.

Before the quilt is marked for quilting, it should be given a final pressing. Press the border seams toward the plain borders.

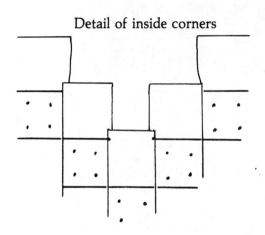

Detail of inside corners

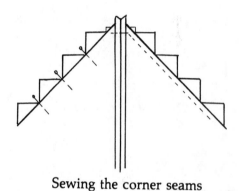

Sewing the corner seams

Attaching
the outer plain border

Attaching
the border sections

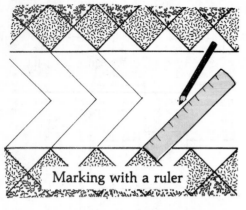
Marking with a ruler

Marking around a template

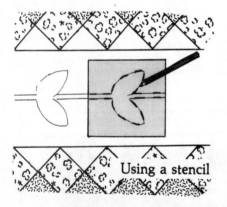
Using a stencil

Using a paper pattern

Marking for Quilting

Always mark with a light touch; quilting is close work so don't mark any darker than is needed. Use a sharp pencil or chalk dressmakers pencil. Basically, there are four different methods for transferring a quilting design from paper to cloth:

Ruler—A ruler or any other straight edge can be used to draw straight line designs. The squares should be marked this way if they are to be quilted from corner to corner.

Template—A cardboard template can be made of simple shapes such as hearts or flowers. Trace around these on the fabric.

Stencil—There are many commercial stencils available. To make your own stencil the design must first be transferred to lightweight cardboard or plastic. Cut slots with a craft knife along the lines of the design. Place the stencil on top of the quilt and mark through the slots with a pencil.

Paper Pattern—With this method, the quilt is placed over a paper quilting pattern and the design is traced on the fabric. Always place something light, such as a piece of posterboard, under the paper pattern to help the lines show. Use a light box for very dark fabrics.

Whichever method is used, it is important to mark the corners of the borders first. Any adjustments to the design can be made toward the center of the border where it will be less noticeable. The design can be spread apart a little or even slightly overlapped.

The quilting patterns in the back of the book have been designed with the repeat of the design the same size as the width. It is possible to turn a corner at any repeat of the design. Some of these patterns have special corner designs. The baby quilts in Plates 8 and 11 show how smoothly the hearts and bows designs continue around the corners.

The wall quilts on the back cover and in Plate 10 feature quilting designs that do not turn the corner. The rest of the border is filled in with straight lines of quilting.

The outer and inner plain borders do not have to use the same quilting pattern. Ruth Green used both feather and cable designs in her quilt in Plate 7. Teen Keith filled in the outer border of her quilt in Plate 6 with simple lines of quilting. It is important, however, that any continuous design turns the corners smoothly.

Basting the Quilt

Prepare the backing by seaming the lengths together with ¾ inch seams. Trim off the selvages, then press the seams open. Cut the backing at least two inches larger than the quilt top on all sides. Cut the batting the same size as the backing.

The layers of the quilt are basted together for quilting on a hoop. It is important that all the layers are kept smooth during the basting. The quilt layers can be spread and taped to the floor for basting. We prefer using a table even though some of the quilt will be draped over the sides. Mark the centers of all the edges of the three layers. This will keep the layers aligned.

Carefully spread the batting on top of the backing. Packaged batting should always be removed from the package the day before and the folds allowed to relax. Place the quilt on top of the batting, smooth out any fullness. Baste in parallel rows, every six inches, using quilting thread and a long, fine needle.

Some quilters prefer double basting. Spread out the batting first, then add the backing on top, face up. Baste in rows, twelve inches apart in one direction only. Turn the layers over and add the top. Baste again in both directions, with rows every six inches.

Since some of the quilts are edged with the patchwork instead of the plain borders, resist the temptation to stretch the quilt.

These outer squares do not have to be trimmed or staystitched. Baste through them carefully; they will be trimmed after the binding is added. For frame quilting, baste muslin strips, or the leftover fabric from the borders, to the outer squares before putting it on the frame.

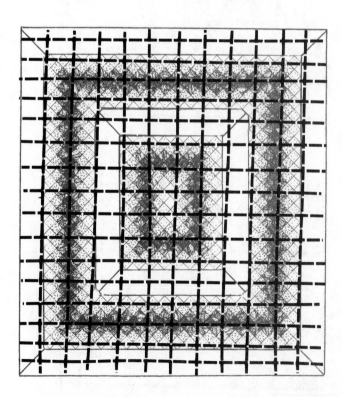

Basting in parallel lines

Traditional quilting

Outline quilting

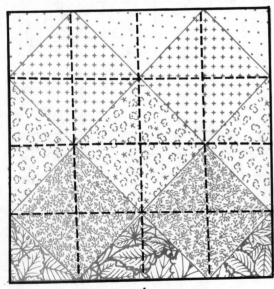

Crossing the square

Quilting the Quilt

The *Boston Commons* quilt offers two types of surface for quilting, the squares and the plain borders. The squares need only simple lines of stitching but the plain borders call for the kind of quilting that will leave them anything but plain! Now is the time to use feathers, cables, interlocking squares, basketweaves; any pattern that you feel will complement the quilt design and show off your skills.

Traditionally, the squares were quilted ¼ inch away from the seams. They can also be outlined, by quilting right next to the seam, or crossed, as in the quilt on the cover.

Adding extra rows of quilting to the background will emphasize the design. More quilting will flatten the background and make the design appear to protrude. The quilt on the front cover is a good example of this. It was originally quilted with the lines through the squares continuing into the feather design. The feather blended in with the lines. After additional lines were quilted, the feather became the focal point.

If a hoop is used, quilt the center section first and work outward. If the quilt is put on a frame for quilting, the outer edges would be quilted first. The quilt in Plate 16 was set up at a quilting bee; the outer border shows the first area that was quilted.

The color of quilting thread can match or contrast the fabric. Using a darker thread will emphasize the stitches. Thread the needle with about 18 inches of quilting thread. We begin and end each line of quilting by tying a single knot in the thread and popping it through the top layer. Take small, even stitches through the three layers. Take several stitches before pulling the needle through. Experiment by using smaller needles; we think you'll find your stitches will also become smaller.

Crossing seams can be a problem because of the extra layers there. Stitch as deep as possible, even if it only catches the top and batting. Skipped stitches on the back can be filled in later.

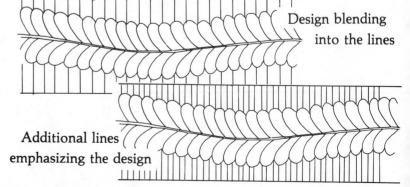

Design blending into the lines

Additional lines emphasizing the design

Binding the Quilt

Since these quilts have a traditional look, we have used a traditional binding. It is narrower than we usually use and will be more in proportion to the small squares. Bias bindings round slightly and the seams are less noticeable than bindings cut on the straight of the fabric. We use a double binding for durability.

Fold the fabric, bringing the cut edge to the selvage to find the bias. Fold again, with the folds together. This makes a smaller piece to handle. Measure and mark the first strip 1½ inches away from the folds. Continue to mark every 3 inches. Cut on the marked lines. Sew these strips together using ½ inch seams. Trim the seam to ¼ inch and press open. Fold the binding in half lengthwise and press. Staystitch the raw edges together, ¼ inch in, without stretching the binding. Leave the first ten inches unstitched.

Sew the binding to all three layers of the quilt. Start in the middle of the bottom edge, leaving the first ten inches free. Stop the stitching ¼ inch away from the edge (or in the center of the corner squares, if the quilt ends with the patchwork border). Make a ½ inch pleat in the corner to form a mitered corner. Reinsert the needle on the other side of the pleat without leaving a gap. Do not sew over the pleat. With the needle in, pivot the quilt and continue sewing.

Stop stitching about twelve inches from the starting point. To join the ends, remove the staystitching and open the binding. Overlap the ends to mark and cut, allowing for seams. Sew the ends together, then finish sewing the binding to the quilt. Trim off any excess backing, and leave an inch of batting. This will pad the binding and help it last longer. Blind stitch the folded edge of the binding to the back of the quilt.

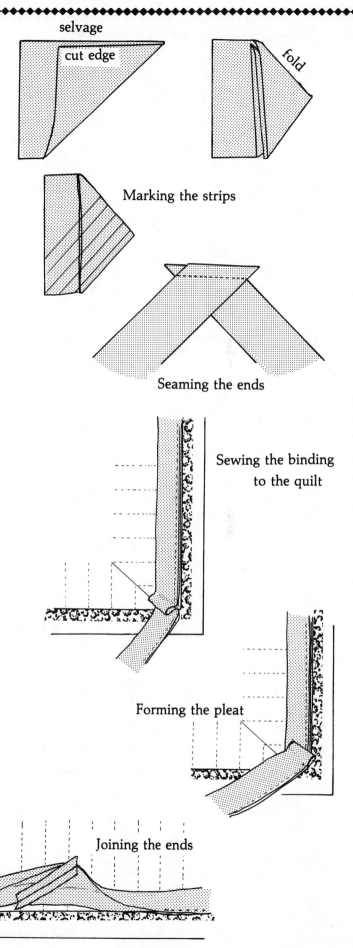

selvage

cut edge

fold

Marking the strips

Seaming the ends

Sewing the binding to the quilt

Forming the pleat

Blindstitching the binding to the quilt back

Joining the ends

Quilt size — 30″ × 34″
Square size — 1-1/4″ (sewn)

Fabric	Amount	Rows
1	5/8 yard	8
2 — 5	1/2 yard each	5 each
Plain borders	1 yard	
Backing	1-1/8 yards	
Binding	1/2 yard	

Fabric 1 is the same fabric as the plain borders.
Size variation—It is possible to make two different sizes of wall quilts using the same sewing layouts and changing the size of the square.

In the wall quilt the top/bottom border sections and the side border sections contain the same number of squares. Use the same sewing layout for all four border sections.

Quilt size — 36″ × 40″
Square size — 1-1/2″ (sewn)

Fabric	Amount	Rows
1	3/4 yard	9
2 — 5	1/2 yard each	6 each
Plain borders	1-1/4 yards	
Backing	1-1/4 yards	
Binding	1/2 yard	

Sewing Layout/Single Row

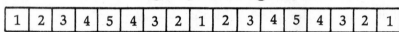

Sewing Layout/Center

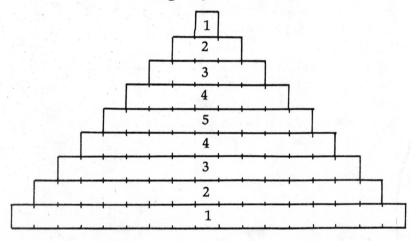

Sewing Layout/Side Borders/Top & Bottom Borders

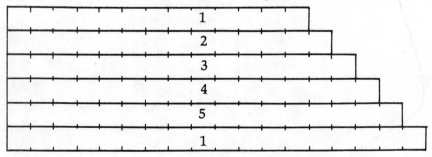

BABY QUILT

Quilt size — 42" × 47"
Square size — 1-1/2" (sewn)

Fabric	Amount	Rows
1 — 4	3/4 yard each	9 each
5	1/2 yard	5
Plain borders	1-1/4 yards	
Backing	1-1/2 yards	
Binding	3/4 yard	

Fabric 1 is the same fabric as the plain borders.

In the baby quilt, the top/bottom border sections and the side border sections contain the same number of squares. Use the same sewing layout for all four border sections.

Sewing Layout/Single Row

1	2	3	4	5	4	3	2	1	2	3	4	5	4	3	2	1

Sewing Layout/Center

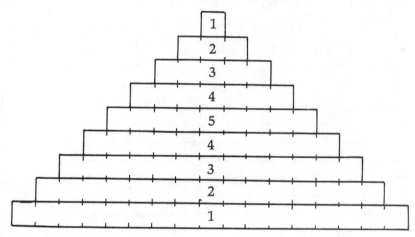

Sewing Layout/Side Borders/Top & Bottom Borders

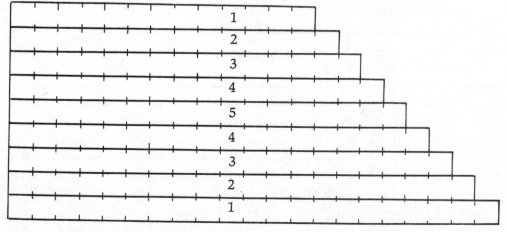

Quilt size — 74" × 96"
Square size — 1-3/4" (sewn)

Fabric 1 is the same fabric as the plain borders.

The twin size quilt is edged with the patch-work border. There is no outer plain border.

Fabric	Amount	Rows
1 — 6	1-1/2 yards each	18 each
7	3/4 yard	9
Plain borders	2-1/4 yards	
Backing	6 yards (2 — 108" lengths)	

Sewing Layout/Center

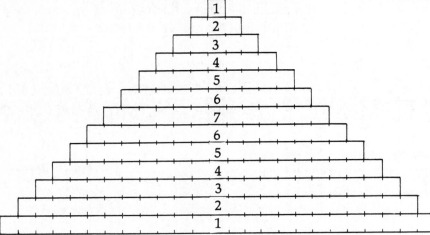

Sewing Layout/Single Rows

Sewing Layout/Top & Bottom Borders

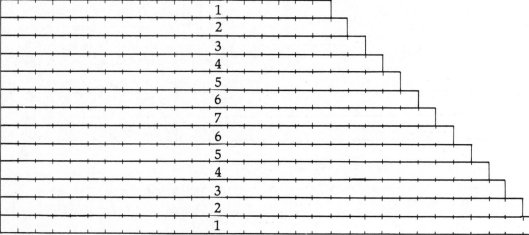

Sewing Layout/Side Borders

34

DOUBLE/QUEEN SIZE QUILT ◆◆◆◆◆◆◆◆◆◆◆◆◆◆◆◆◆◆◆◆◆◆◆◆◆◆◆◆◆◆◆

Quilt size — 89″ × 104″
Square size — 1-3/4″ (sewn)

Fabric	Amount	Rows
1 — 6	1-1/4 yards each	16
7	3/4 yard	8
Plain borders	5 yards	
Backing	9-1/4 yards (3 — 111″ lengths)	
Binding	1-1/4 yards	

Fabric 1 is the same fabric as the plain borders.

Size variation—The Double/Queen size quilt will measure 74″ × 89″ if the outer plain border is eliminated. Purchase 2 yards of the plain border fabric for the inner plain borders.

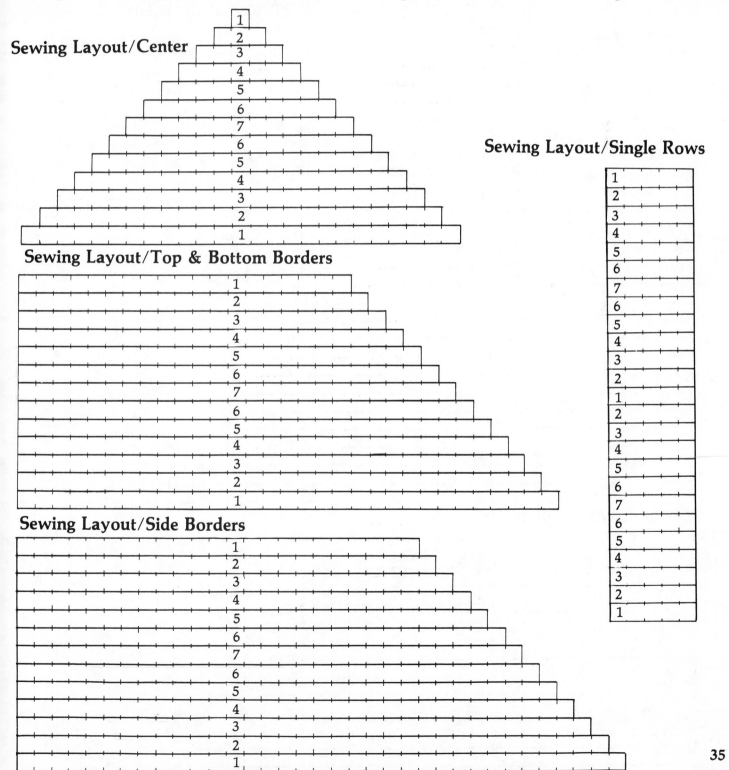

Sewing Layout/Center

Sewing Layout/Top & Bottom Borders

Sewing Layout/Side Borders

Sewing Layout/Single Rows

Quilt size — 102″ X 110″
Square size — 2″ (sewn)

Fabric	Amount	Rows
1 — 6	1-1/2 yards each	17 each
7	3/4 yard	9
Plain borders	5-1/4 yards	
Backing	9-3/4 yards	(3 — 117″ lengths)
Binding	1-1/4 yards	

Fabric 1 is the same fabric as the plain borders.
Size variation—The King size quilt will measure 85″ × 93″ if the outer plain border is eliminated. Purchase 2-1/8 yards of the plain border fabric for the inner plain borders.

Sewing Layout/Center

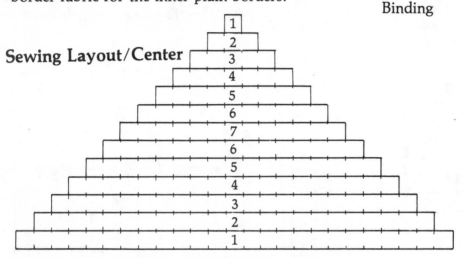

Sewing Layout/Single Row

Sewing Layout/Top & Bottom Borders

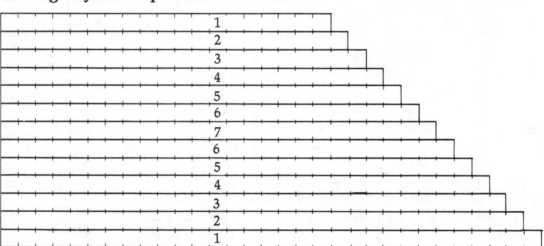

Sewing Layout/Side Borders

36